T0108222

LITTLE LEGENDS ALPHABET

Words by Robin Feiner

NASA
NASA
ALYSSA CARSON

Aa

A is for Alyssa Carson. From the age of three, Alyssa dreamed of one day going to space. Now in her teens, NASA has decided she's got 'the right stuff'... they're training her for a mission to Mars. In 2033, she could be the first person to step foot on the Red Planet.

B

B is for Millie Bobby Brown. Once called 'the world's most famous 12-year-old,' this amazing British actor and model is now one of the most influential teens. With close ties to UNICEF and other charities, she admirably puts all that influence to good use.

C is for **C**laudette Colvin.
In segregated Alabama,
at the age of 15, Claudette
stood her ground and
refused to give up her seat
on a bus. This was nine
months before Rosa Parks
famously did the same.
What a legendary pioneer
of the civil rights movement.

Dd

D is for Laura Dekker.
At the age of 16, this New Zealand-born Dutch sailor bravely and ambitiously set sail. After 518 grueling days at sea, she became the youngest person to circumnavigate the globe single-handed. Ahoy there, legend!

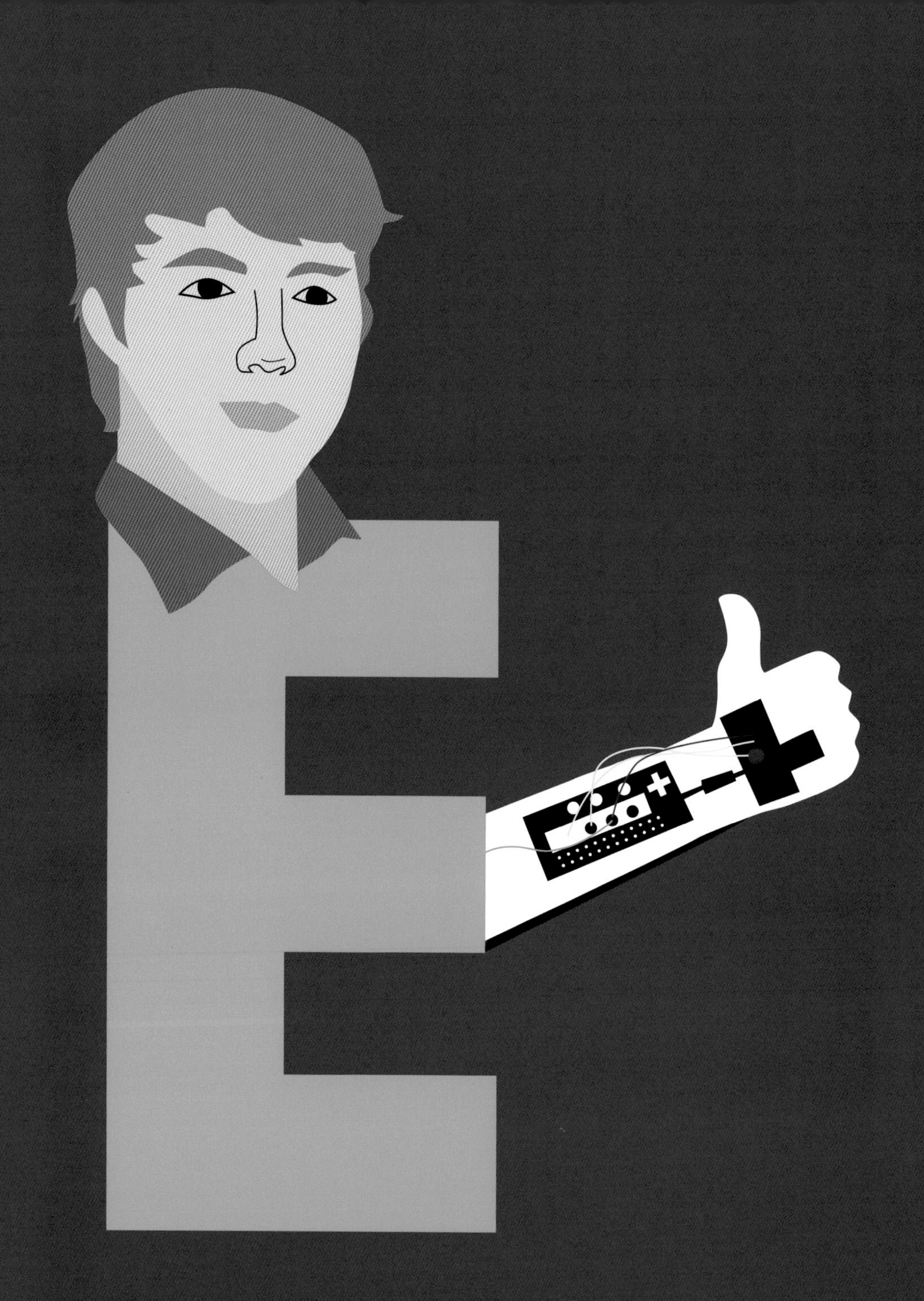

Ee

E is for Easton LaChappelle. As a 14-year-old inventor, Easton decided to build a remote-controlled robotic hand. At 17, he was invited to the White House, where he used his incredible invention – RoboArm – to shake Obama's hand. What a whiz-kid!

F is for Anne **F**rank. Her childhood diary, written while hiding from the Nazis during World War II, is now a celebrated book translated into over 60 languages. Understanding her fears and bravery helps ensure the world never forgets.

Gg

G is for Gregory Smith. Pledging his life to world peace and the plight of underprivileged children, this little legend has met world leaders, spoken before the UN, and earned a Nobel Peace Prize nomination, all by age 12.

Hh

H is for Ryan Hreljac.
By the age of seven, this Canadian had established Ryan's Well Foundation. With over 1000 wells dug, they now bring clean water to over 800,000 people in Africa and around the world.

Ii

I is for Iqbal Masih.
A child slave in Pakistan since the age of four, he bravely escaped when he was 10. Thanks to his activism and powerful speeches around the world, 'the little hero' helped free thousands enslaved like him.

J is for Joan of Arc.
In medieval France, an unknown teenage peasant girl led the French army to victory over the English, ending the Hundred Years' War. Now a symbolic figure of France, 'The Maid of Orléans' is the subject of many films, paintings, books and plays.

Kk

K is for Chloe Kim. Learning to snowboard as a four-year-old, Chloe was competing by the age of six. At 17, she'd become the youngest woman to ever win gold at the Olympics in the Half Pipe. This Korean American's legendary skills will give you chills.

Ll

L is for Louis Braille. Blinded by an accident when very young, this brilliant French boy mastered his disability and studied very hard at a special school for the blind. While still a student there, he invented Braille, a system that allows the blind to read and write. Genius!

M is for Maya Penn.
This dynamic American entrepreneur is on a quest to create jobs and save the planet. She launched her eco-friendly fashion house at the age of eight and her non-profit company shortly after. Maya is a little business woman with one big future.

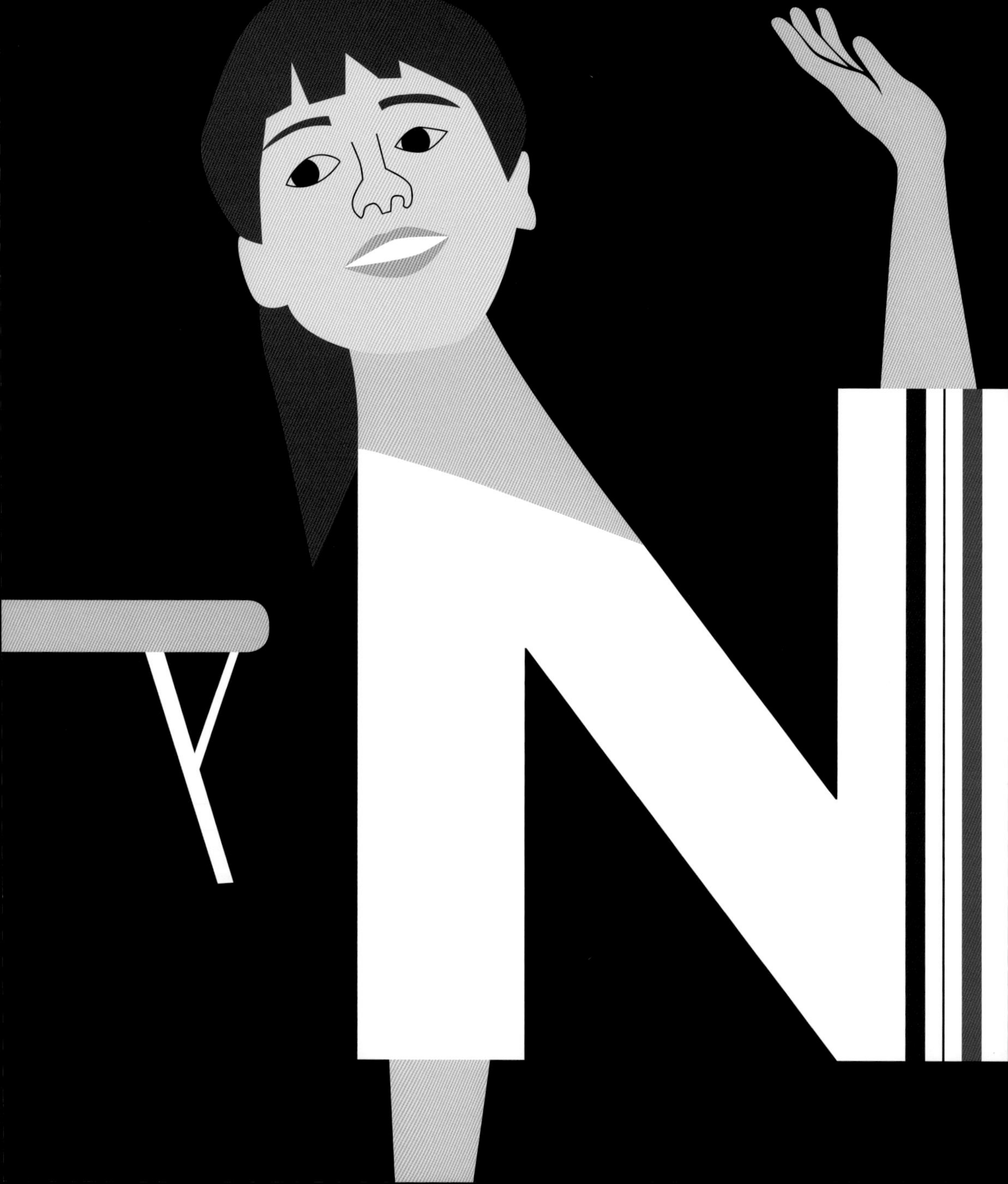

Nn

N is for Nadia Comăneci. While only 14 years old, this legendary Romanian gymnast dazzled the world. At the '76 Montreal Olympic Games she became the first Olympian to ever score a perfect 10. She also won five Olympic gold medals.

Oo

O is for Emmanuel Ofosu Yeboah. As one of many disabled orphans living in Ghana, he decided to bring attention to their struggle. With only one strong leg, he rode a bike across his country. The documentary, Emmanuel's Gift, tells this little legend's incredible story.

P

Pp

P is for **P**hilo Farnsworth. This little inventor had a very big idea. In his 14-year-old mind, Philo Farnsworth had invented the television. With some help from his Chemistry teacher and a lot of hard work, he transmitted his first electronic images seven years later.

Q is for Anna Paquin.
At age 11, with little acting experience, this New Zealand-Canadian scored a dream role in a wonderful film called, The Piano. Her performance stunned critics and earned her an Oscar - one of the youngest to ever receive this accolade. Bravo!

Rr

R is for Jordan Romero. Jordan always had his sights set high. At just 13, inspired by a painting of the world's seven tallest mountains, he became the youngest person to conquer Everest. He then went on to become the youngest person to conquer all seven peaks.

S

S is for Boyan **S**lat.
With a World Record for water rocket launching at age 14, it was clear Boyan was special. By 16, he'd come up with a radical idea for cleaning up our oceans. That idea has captured the world's attention and won him the Champions of the Earth award.

T is for Thandiwe Chama. Believing that every child, not just the wealthy, has a right to an education, she's been tirelessly fighting for better educational opportunities in Zambia since she was eight. Her bravery and dedication has earned her the International Children's Peace Prize.

Uu

U is for Mikaila Ulmer. After being stung by a bee, a 10-year-old Mikaila was saddened to learn that honey bee numbers were dwindling. By 11, she had created a company that sells honey-sweetened lemonade to help save the bees. What a buzz!

V is for Winter Vinecki.
The youngest person to complete marathons on seven different continents, this little sports legend was then crowned IronKids triathlon champion. While raising the bar, Winter also raises money for cancer research. Go Team Winter!

W

W is for Stevie **W**onder.
At the age of 11, a young blind piano player called Stevland Morris was taken for an audition at Motown Records. He was instantly declared a child prodigy, given a record deal and dubbed Little Stevie Wonder.

Xx

X is for Alex Scott.
As a four-year-old bravely
battling cancer, she decided
she wanted to raise money
to help other kids like her.
Within a few years, Alex saw
her lemonade stand raise
over one million dollars.
She will be remembered
as a brave little legend.

Yy

Y is for Malala Yousafzai. From an early age, this Pakistani activist campaigned fearlessly for the education of under-privileged women. She famously became the youngest winner of the Nobel Peace Prize and one of the biggest little legends in history.

Zz

Z is for Maddie Ziegler.
This incredible kid is most famous for her mesmerizing dance performances on a series of pop music videos. In fact, she's danced her way into Time magazine's 'Influential Teens' list three years in a row. Maddie, take a bow.